Series editor: Tim Carr

BIBLE SOCIETY
Stonehill Green, Westlea, SWINDON SN5 7DG, England

First published 1991

British Library Cataloguing in Publication Data
Parsons, Jeni
Women in the World
1. Bible. Special Subjects. Society. Role of Women
I. Title II. Bible Society III. Series
220.830542

ISBN 0–564–05975–7

Printed in Great Britain by Stanley L. Hunt (Printers) Ltd, Rushden, Northants

Bible Societies exist to provide resources for Bible distribution and use. Bible Society in England and Wales (BFBS) is a member of the United Bible Societies, an international partnership working in over 180 countries. Their common aim is to reach all people with the Bible, or some part of it, in a language they can understand and at a price they can afford. Parts of the Bible have now been translated into approximately 1900 languages. Bible Societies aim to help every church at every point where it uses the Bible. You are invited to share in this work by your prayers and gifts. The Bible Society in your country will be very happy to provide details of its activity.

How to use this book

The six sessions all follow a similar pattern of individual preparation, group study and prayer, outlined here.

Preparation before the meeting

Read the material for the session carefully. You may find it helpful to read the Bible passages aloud so that you can hear the story and its detail rather than just skim it. The preparation for each week is at the end of the previous session (except for Session One). This gives you a chance to look at what there is to prepare for the next time you meet, and to divide the practical tasks among the group if it is appropriate. Make notes of any ideas or questions you have about the subjects so that you can raise them at the group meeting.

Group study

Take to the group meeting this book, a Bible and a pencil and anything else that the preparation notes ask for. Be willing to share your thoughts and ideas. Even if you think one of your ideas is a a bit "way out", risk putting it in because someone else may find it helpful and it could trigger deeper thought in the group. At the same time, be sure that everyone gets a chance to have their say and that no one dominates the group.

People are not in the group to criticize one another but to share in Christian discipleship and learning; and that means listening as well as speaking. If the members of the group are to trust each other, anything discussed must be treated as a matter of confidentiality. Sometimes a particular exercise will be suggested which will be new to you. Give it a try and see what you learn.

Prayer

At the end of each session there is a prayer by Janet Morley which relates to the theme you have already discussed. Allow time for the words to sink in, and use the suggestions for meditation to help you listen to God speaking through the discussion and calling you on to renewed discipleship.

For the group leader

The studies can be led by the same person, or different individuals (or pairs) each time. Each of these sessions works on its own, and they do not need to be taken in the order in which they are set. However, the order has been arranged so that participants share more deeply each time and can learn more about one another as they go. There are exercises which may be new to some group members but in doing them a lot can be learned, so be prepared to give gentle encouragement for those who aren't sure. The exercises are a good way to help individuals and the group as a whole to learn, so it is better not to miss them out or the sessions won't work as well.

Practical points

† Be sure that everyone knows where the meeting will be and at what time it will begin and end. The studies are designed to last about 1½ hours and people will be more

willing to attend regularly if they know that there is a set finishing time.

- † Be sure that any equipment needed will be on hand (scissors, glue, paper, etc.).
- † Make sure the room is light enough and that there are enough chairs for everyone. It is also a good idea to check things like heat and ventilation so that everyone is comfortable.

Leading group study

Make sure everyone knows each other's name if people have not met before, and take some time for them to introduce themselves if yours is a new group. Lead the group through the session material, making sure everyone gets an opportunity to speak and that no one dominates – not even you! At the end of the session confirm the time, date and place of the next meeting, and who is going to be leading it. Encourage people to stay and talk, perhaps over a cup of tea or coffee, if they have time. If someone has to miss a group meeting, try to explain a little of what happened to them so that they don't lose the thread of the set of studies. If a session arouses strong emotions in a participant, be sensitive and encourage the other group members to listen. However, try not to get sidetracked away from the material for the session for too long; as a group leader you will have to balance the needs of the individual and the group. If necessary, take time after the session to listen further so that the person knows they have been heard by someone, and does not leave with the feelings still "bottled up".

Introduction

Women have always occupied a place in the world but have often been invisible to the writers of history unless there was some particular reason to point out their existence. Working people, too, have experience of the fact that history describes the lives and activities of, for example, the monarchy, generals and important politicians, and leaves their lives out of account. In British society today women are more visible in work, leadership and power than they have been previously, a position that has been achieved by the many women in the past before us who refused to remain invisible.

These studies set out to explore just some of the many situations in which we find ourselves, using the Bible to help highlight issues for us. We can begin to root ourselves in the Bible in new ways so that the stories and experiences of women and men in the Bible come alive and help us to interpret our own experience. In these studies you will find different ways, for example, using pictures, clay, new prayers and your own stories, to enable you to look more deeply at what God calls you to be and to do in the world.

Even as people of the late twentieth century, we can look at our experiences of life in the light of the Bible Story, finding that God is there in our joy and also the pain and defeat. We may be sure that God is there, but often we need the company and the reflection of others with whom we can discuss and compare our story, feelings and thoughts. Group Bible study is particularly important as a help for Christian living in this complex and exciting world. Your group will have an advantage if it is made up of people who reflect the variety of your local community. This diverse mix is a cause for both rejoicing and pain in our society, and it is possible to gain a lot from others who have different view points to our own. Hearing different perspectives is necessary if the gospel is to be proclaimed to all people. Some groups will have a mixture of women and men and this too can be a chance for everyone to learn. However, these studies are concerned to look at women's experience in the world and therefore take that focus.

The six areas of study are based on women's lives in the world.

- † We begin by looking at images of women in the world which we shall explore through the two accounts of creation in the book of Genesis. Through these we can examine our creation in the likeness of God and what that can mean.
- † The second session focuses on the roles that women take in the world of work, both waged and unwaged. Looking at some features of women's work in childbirth, housekeeping and also in discipleship, we can see the liberating attitude that Jesus had towards the women he met.
- † In the third study the theme will be that of leadership. Through reflection on the model of the leader as servant, we can look at women's experience of leadership and service.
- † The fourth session looks at the issue of sexuality, and through the love poetry of the Song of Songs we can see how women have been not only the objects of another's sexuality but also active in describing their own desires. We shall then look at Jesus' own reactions to the physical nature of women.
- † In the fifth session we shall give time to the theme of God's creation, and consider the environment and our need to care for it.
- † Finally we shall consider the theme of justice in this country and also in the wider world. Women have

greater economic power in the Western world than in the past and this session will look at how everyone may be involved in struggles for justice today.

Being a woman in the world means that life is complex and full of challenge. Through the Bible we can hear the unmistakable call of God to be active for the Kingdom of God. Studying the Bible and sharing personal experiences together in a group will give us the strength to pursue God's call to discipleship, and the courage to stand together as women and men with greater understanding of one another and of God.

SESSION ONE

IMAGES OF WOMEN

AIM

In this session you will begin to explore what it means to be made in the image of God, and yet at the same time be surrounded in the world by so many conflicting images of women. You will be asked to think what it is about you that reflects God's image. You will also consider where the images of women come from that the world presents: who is telling women what they must be like?

PREPARATION FOR THIS SESSION

We are surrounded by images of women, both in art and in advertizing. In preparation for the group meeting, try to watch some of the adverts on television and note the images of women shown. In particular note their age, their colour, their class, what they are doing and anything else that catches your attention. Take a magazine and cut out pictures of women and girls that reflect what you have seen on television and take them with you to the meeting. Take a photograph of yourself as well if you can.

Read through the following passages aloud. Write down any feelings you had about these passages as you read them. If you have time, compare the three passages and note the similarities and the differences.

26 Then God said, "And now we will make human beings; they will be like us and resemble us. They will have power over the fish, the birds, and all animals, domestic and wild, large and small." 27 So

*God created human beings, making
them to be like himself. He created
them male and female, [28]blessed
them, and said, "Have many chil-
dren, so that your descendants will
live all over the earth and bring it
under their control. I am putting
you in charge of the fish, the birds,
and all the wild animals. [29]I have
provided all kinds of grain and all
kinds of fruit for you to eat; [30]but
for all the wild animals and for all
the birds I have provided grass and
leafy plants for food" – and it was
done. [31]God looked at everything
he had made, and he was very
pleased. Evening passed and morn-
ing came – that was the sixth day.*

Genesis 1.26–31

*[7]Then the LORD God took some
soil from the ground and formed a
man out of it; he breathed life-
giving breath into his nostrils and
the man began to live.*

*[8]Then the LORD God planted a
garden in Eden, in the East, and
there he put the man he had
formed. [9]He made all kinds of
beautiful trees grow there and pro-
duce good fruit. In the middle of the
garden stood the tree that gives life
and the tree that gives knowledge of
what is good and what is bad.*

Genesis 2.7–9

*[15]Then the LORD God placed the
man in the Garden of Eden to culti-
vate it and guard it. [16]He said to
him, "You may eat the fruit of any
tree in the garden, [17]except the tree
that gives knowledge of what is
good and what is bad. You must
not eat the fruit of that tree; if you
do, you will die the same day."*

*[18]Then the LORD God said, "It is
not good for the man to live alone. I
will make a suitable companion to
help him." [19]So he took some soil
from the ground and formed all the
animals and all the birds. Then he
brought them to the man to see what
he would name them; and that is
how they all got their names. [20]So
the man named all the birds and all
the animals; but not one of them
was a suitable companion to help
him.*

*[21]Then the LORD God made the
man fall into a deep sleep, and
while he was sleeping, he took out
one of the man's ribs and closed up
the flesh. [22]He formed a woman out
of the rib and brought her to him.
[23]Then the man said,*

*"At last, here is one of my own
kind –
Bone taken from my bone, and
flesh from my flesh.
'Woman' is her name because
she was taken out of man."*

*[24]That is why a man leaves his
father and mother and is united
with his wife, and they become one.*

*[25]The man and the woman were
both naked, but they were not
embarrassed.*

Genesis 2.15–25

Genesis 1.26–31 is part of the first account of creation (the second account is in Genesis chapter 2). This Good News Bible translation uses the term "human beings" in verse 26; but you may be familiar with other translations that say "man" instead. Some people, particularly some women, are put off by language that uses masculine words like "man" for both sexes. They prefer more "inclusive" language (like "human beings") to cover both men and women. Be aware that the use of exclusive language may actually be a source of pain for some members of your group, even if it is not for you. The first account of creation emphasizes that both men and women are created by God in God's own image, and it is this that we shall concentrate on in this section. In the second passage God recognizes the aloneness of the man, and after searching among the animals and birds for a "suitable companion to help him", God takes part of the man to create the woman. It is worth noting that God does not form the woman from the dust as God had formed the man, the animals and the birds, but rather of living flesh and bone. She is not a separate species but intimately related to the man.

Group Study

- † In twos or threes spend some time discussing the three passages from Genesis that you have already read, and note each other's reactions. Do you agree in your feelings?
- † In the main group discuss what it means to each of you to be made in the image of God. What is it about God and you that is the same? You might like to end this part of the session by going round the group saying, "I'm (first name), and I'm made in God's image." As a group you may need to give a fair amount of time to this before

moving on to the next part, since it is often a new thought for some women.

- † Pool all your cuttings from the magazines and discuss what sort of women are shown. How does this relate to TV adverts?
- † What sort of women are missing? Are they missing in your group?
- † Stick all the pictures on a large sheet of paper leaving some space in the middle. Stick a photograph of each group member in the middle and also write in any particular group of women who are missing, e.g. black women, old women, very young women, disabled women. Write on the top of the sheet "All made in God's image."
- † Consider your poster and discuss where the dominant images come from – reality, the advertizers, ourselves? Who controls what the acceptable images of women are in our society?

PRAYER

Spend the final part of the group in silence meditating on your poster and thanking God for the variety of women and their likeness to God. Pray for the others in your group and then say together:

God our Lover,

You draw us to search for you;
you give us clues to your presence in creation;
we find you in each other's faces,
in the challenge and the intimacy of human love.
Yet always you elude our grasp;
familiar and yet always strange,

you both comfort and disturb our
lives.
We surrender all our images of you,
and offer ourselves to your darkness;
that you may enable us to become
your likeness
more than we can imagine or
conceive.

Amen.

PREPARATION FOR SESSION TWO

Before the meeting make a list of all the areas of work you do, both paid and unpaid, not forgetting the "invisible" work of raising children, caring for relatives or neighbours, home-making and so on. See if you can find any statistics about women's work in this country or other countries (try your local library or trade union), and take them with your list to the group session. The following may give you a start:

> UNICEF records that women form 50% of the world's population, do 66% of the recognized work, receive 10% of the world's income and own less than 1% of the world's property.

SESSION TWO

WOMEN AND WORK

AIM

In this session you will begin to explore your experiences of women's work, both waged and unwaged, and to reflect on attitudes in the Bible to what is traditionally perceived as women's work.

[14]Then the LORD God said to the
snake, "You will be punished for
this; you alone of all the animals
must bear this curse: From now on
you will crawl on your belly, and
you will have to eat dust as long as
you live. [15]I will make you and the
woman hate each other; her
offspring and yours will always be
enemies. Her offspring will crush
your head, and you will bite their
heel."
[16]And he said to the woman,
"I will increase your trouble in
pregnancy and your pain in giving
birth. In spite of this, you will still
have desire for your husband, yet
you will be subject to him."
[17]And he said to the man, "You
listened to your wife and ate the
fruit which I told you not to eat.
Because of what you have done, the
ground will be under a curse. You
will have to work hard all your life
to make it produce enough food for
you. [18]It will produce weeds and
thorns, and you will have to eat
wild plants. [19]You will have to work
hard and sweat to make the soil
produce anything, until you go
back to the soil from which you
were formed. You were made from
soil, and you will become soil
again."
[20]Adam named his wife Eve, be-
cause she was the mother of all
human beings. [21]And the LORD
God made clothes out of animal
skins for Adam and his wife, and he
clothed them.

Genesis 3.14–21

[38]As Jesus and his disciples went on
their way, he came to a village
where a woman named Martha wel-
comed him in her home. [39]She had
a sister named Mary, who sat down
at the feet of the Lord and listened

to his teaching. [40] *Martha was upset over all the work she had to do, so she came and said, "Lord, don't you care that my sister has left me to do all the work by myself? Tell her to come and help me!"*
[41] *The Lord answered her, "Martha, Martha! You are worried and troubled over so many things,*
[42] *but just one is needed. Mary has chosen the right thing, and it will not be taken away from her."*

Luke 10.38–42

The Genesis story describes the results of the disobedience of Eve, Adam and the snake in the garden. Each will have to struggle not only with the others but also with his or her environment and future. The woman and the man will have to labour hard in their different ways and live without equality and also without intimacy with God (Genesis 3.23–24). There is a discussion about roles in the story from Luke where Jesus meets Mary and Martha. In five short verses the author captures a debate that will be familiar to many people who experience the hard work of housekeeping and who struggle with priorities – in this case between caring for human, physical needs and hearing about the Good News of the Kingdom, where God will meet all needs.

Group Study

- † In twos or threes share your lists of work, paid and unpaid, that you do. Then discuss the Genesis passage and its explanation of why women and men have to labour so hard.
- † In the main group talk about whether you could imagine a world without the hard work of childbirth, manual labour and intellectual effort.
- † Talk about where you see God involved in your own work.
- † Divide the group into two halves for ten minutes, one

half to discuss Mary's role in the story in Luke, and the other half to look at Martha's role. Then in the main group using the characters of Mary and Martha, yet being yourselves, discuss how Mary and Martha felt in the story and how they might have responded to Jesus' words.

† Finally, pool any statistics you have found about women workers in the world.
What do these figures say to you as a group?

Prayer

Pray for the women and men whose work is seemingly without reward or recognition, and who are broken by their labour. Pray for the strength to challenge the oppression that results. Pray together:

O God, the power of the powerless,
you have chosen as your witnesses
those whose voice is not heard.
Grant that, as women first announced
the Resurrection
though they were not believed,
we too may have courage
to persist in proclaiming your word,
In the power of Jesus Christ, Amen.

Preparation for Session Three

Before the session make a list of women who were in leadership positions in the Bible. There are quite a few in the Old Testament. Those in the New Testament are often mentioned by Paul at the beginning or end of his letters. Make a list of the leadership tasks in your local community and in your church, and see how many women are involved in them. Take the lists with you to the group meeting.

SESSION THREE

WOMEN AND LEADERSHIP

AIM

In this session, through two passages from the Gospels, you will look at the sort of leadership which Jesus commended. Both of them involve the washing of feet. By reflecting on the twin notions of leadership and service you will look further at women's experience in the light of the gospel.

[36]A Pharisee invited Jesus to have
dinner with him, and Jesus went to
his house and sat down to eat. [37] In
that town was a woman who lived a
sinful life. She heard that Jesus was
eating in the Pharisee's house, so
she brought an alabaster jar full of
perfume [38]and stood behind Jesus,
by his feet, crying and wetting his
feet with her tears. Then she dried
his feet with her hair, kissed them,
and poured the perfume on them.
[39]When the Pharisee saw this, he
said to himself, "If this man really
were a prophet, he would know
who this woman is who is touching
him; he would know what kind of
sinful life she lives!"
[40]Jesus spoke up and said to him,
"Simon, I have something to tell
you."
"Yes, Teacher," he said, "tell
me."
[41]"There were two men who
owed money to a money-lender,"
Jesus began. "One owed him five
hundred silver coins, and the other
owed him fifty. [42]Neither of them
could pay him back, so he cancelled
the debts of both. Which one, then,
will love him more?"
[43]"I suppose," answered Simon,
"that it would be the one who was
forgiven more."
"You are right," said Jesus.
[44]Then he turned to the woman and
said to Simon, "Do you see this
woman? I came into your home,
and you gave me no water for my
feet, but she has washed my feet
with her tears and dried them with
her hair. [45]You did not welcome me
with a kiss, but she has not stopped
kissing my feet since I came. [46]You
provided no olive-oil for my head,
but she has covered my feet with

perfume. [17]I tell you, then, the great love she has shown proves that her many sins have been forgiven. But whoever has been forgiven little shows only a little love."

[48]Then Jesus said to the woman, "Your sins are forgiven."

[49]The others sitting at the table began to say to themselves, "Who is this, who even forgives sins?"

[50]But Jesus said to the woman, "Your faith has saved you; go in peace."

Luke 7.36–50

[1]It was now the day before the Passover Festival. Jesus knew that the hour had come for him to leave this world and go to the Father. He had always loved those in the world who were his own, and he loved them to the very end.

[2]Jesus and his disciples were at supper. The Devil had already put into the heart of Judas, the son of Simon Iscariot, the thought of betraying Jesus. [3]Jesus knew that the Father had given him complete power; he knew that he had come from God and was going to God. [4]So he rose from the table, took off his outer garment, and tied a towel round his waist. [5]Then he poured some water into a basin and began to wash the disciples' feet and dry them with the towel round his waist. [6]He came to Simon Peter, who said to him, "Are you going to wash my feet, Lord?"

[7]Jesus answered him, "You do not understand now what I am doing, but you will understand later."

[8]Peter declared, "Never at any time will you wash my feet!"

"If I do not wash your feet," Jesus answered, "you will no longer be my disciple."

[9]Simon Peter answered, "Lord, do not wash only my feet, then! Wash my hands and head, too!"

[10]Jesus said, "Anyone who has had a bath is completely clean and does not have to wash himself, except for his feet. All of you are clean – all except one." [11](Jesus already knew who was going to betray him; that is why he said, "All of you, except one, are clean.")

[12]After Jesus had washed their feet, he put his outer garment back on and returned to his place at the table. "Do you understand what I have just done to you?" he asked. [13]"You call me Teacher and Lord, and it is right that you do so, because that is what I am. [14]I, your Lord and Teacher, have just washed your feet. You, then, should wash one another's feet. [15]I have set an example for you, so that you will do just what I have done for you. [16]I am telling you the truth: no slave is greater than his master, and no messenger is greater than the one who sent him. [17]Now that you know this truth, how happy you will be if you put it into practice!

John 13.1–17

When we read the story of Jesus and Simon the Pharisee today we lose some of the shock value it would have had at the time it happened. Simon was a respected religious leader who honoured Jesus by inviting him to dinner. The shock lies both in Jesus being touched by a woman whose sinful life was well known and in his acceptance of the way she ministered to him, and his criticism of Simon. Through the parable, Jesus describes the woman's extravagant act (for the perfume was extremely expensive) as displaying her love for him; it was far more than Simon did. There are parallels to this story in Matthew 26.6–13 and Mark 14.3–9.

The foot-washing in John's Gospel, in part at least, indicates the form that leadership takes among Jesus' disciples (verse 14). The Gospel writer makes clear the status he believes Jesus to have and then describes the most menial act of service done by him for his disciples. The self-giving act in John's Gospel appears in place of the description of the Last Supper which the other three Gospels describe. The leadership here in the faithful community is one of service rather than of "standing up at the front".

Group Study

† Let the whole group pool the names of biblical leaders who were women. (You might want to look back to the idea of the "invisibility" of women in Session One if you are surprised at how few you know.) Write the names on a big sheet of paper and underline those from the New Testament.

† What characteristics do you think these women had? Certainly you can spot how unusual they were in a male-led society.

† In twos or threes compare your lists of those women who

exercise leadership in your local community and church. What characteristics do these women have?

† Both Gospel stories describe the idea of servanthood, and Christian leadership is sometimes described as being the "servant of the servants of God". Women know all too well the role of serving others. As a group, discuss whether God wants women to be different sorts of leaders from men, and also whether the characteristics Jesus looks to his disciples to show are those more often expected of women.

† Divide into three groups, one to look at the role of Simon the Pharisee, one to look at the role of the woman, and the third to look at the role of the other guests in Luke. In your separate groups talk about the reactions that the person would have had to the incident. After 15 minutes come back together again and discuss what you have learned about leadership from the story. Is the leader always the most important person? Is the leader the one who takes the initiative even for a short time? What is your own leadership role within your local community or church?

PRAYER

Pray for those in "up front" leadership in your local community and church. Pray too for those whose contribution is smaller, but still vital in the advance of God's Kingdom. Pray together:

God our Life-Giver
Again and again we find ourselves
stuck
in old patterns of domination and
submission;
we stay resenting our powerlessness

or guilt-ridden by our power.

Give us courage to believe that
change is possible:
let us so wash one another's feet as
friends
that the fragrance of our ministry may
fill the whole church;
and free us with the symbol of slavery
to make a world where no-one is in
bondage.
In the name of the one who died to
give us life,
Jesus Christ.

Amen

Preparation for Session Four

Before the session, read aloud the passage from Song of Songs on page 22. Do you think it should be included in the Bible? Give reasons for your decision. Then read the passage from Luke 8 on page 23, and think about your own experience of periods, or that of someone who is close to you. Are there taboos in your own community about menstruation? Be prepared to share some of this in the group study.

At the meeting you will need a chopping board, an old newspaper, and some dough or clay (about ½–1 lb).*

* To make play dough, mix 1 lb plain flour with 5 oz salt, and add ⅓ pint water. (Alter the amounts as necessary.)

SESSION FOUR

WOMEN AND SEXUALITY

AIM

In this session you will begin to focus on positive images of sexuality, and on Jesus' tender compassion for the woman whose physical condition kept her apart from the rest of the Jewish community.

10 My lover is handsome and strong;
he is one in ten thousand.
11 His face is bronzed and smooth;
his hair is wavy,
black as a raven.
12 His eyes are as beautiful as doves by a flowing brook,
doves washed in milk and standing by the stream.
13 His cheeks are as lovely as a garden that is full of herbs and spices.
His lips are like lilies, wet with liquid myrrh.
14 His hands are well-formed, and he wears rings set with gems.
His body is like smooth ivory, with sapphires set in it.
15 His thighs are columns of alabaster set in sockets of gold.
He is majestic, like the Lebanon Mountains
with their towering cedars.
16 His mouth is sweet to kiss;
everything about him enchants me.
This is what my lover is like,
women of Jerusalem.

Song of Songs 5.10–16

40 When Jesus returned to the other side of the lake, the people welcomed him, because they had all been waiting for him.
41 Then a man named Jairus arrived; he was an official in the local synagogue. He threw himself down at Jesus' feet and begged him to go to his home,
42 because his only daughter, who was twelve years old, was dying.

As Jesus went along, the people were crowding him from every side.
43 Among them was a woman who had suffered from severe bleeding

for twelve years; she had spent all she had on doctors, but no one had been able to cure her. [44]*She came up in the crowd behind Jesus and touched the edge of his cloak, and her bleeding stopped at once.* [45]*Jesus asked, "Who touched me?"*

Everyone denied it, and Peter said, "Master, the people are all round you and crowding in on you."

[46]*But Jesus said, "Someone touched me, for I knew it when power went out of me."* [47]*The woman saw that she had been found out, so she came trembling and threw herself at Jesus' feet. There in front of everybody, she told him why she had touched him and how she had been healed at once.* [48]*Jesus said to her, "My daughter, your faith has made you well. Go in peace."*

Luke 8.40–48

The sexuality of many women in the Bible has been seen by some to be suspect, and often a source of sin for men – look, for example, at Eve, Jezebel, Delilah, and Gomer. The *Songs of Songs* is a book of ancient love poetry which was finally included among the books of the Bible after a heated debate. It celebrates not only the more usual male appreciation of the physical appearance of women, but also a woman's delight in the attractions of her male lover. The whole book has been read as an allegory of the love between God and the people of Israel, and that interpretation sheds light on the exuberance of love to be felt between God and those who belong to God. Yet taking *Song of Songs* in a literal way as a celebration of human sexuality allows us to find the goodness – the "Godness" – of those personal elements which are rarely mentioned in church or even in our Christian study groups.

The story of Jesus and the woman likewise raises subjects rarely mentioned in such circles either – such as the uterine haemorrhage which this woman may have suffered from. Here, Jesus breaks the taboos of his culture and while on his way to heal Jairus' daughter, he stops and tends to the woman whose courage and faith lead to her own healing. This story can be seen to be about women's sexuality in a more complete way than it first appears. The woman has been excluded from the community for twelve years because her bleeding made her unclean. Jesus is not afraid of the woman's illness even though it makes him temporarily unclean in the eyes of those around him. Jairus' daughter is twelve years old – the age of her religious and sexual maturing. Again, Jesus is prepared to be associated with her. The two passages show how sexuality can exclude – as in the woman with bleeding, and include – as in the girl becoming an adult.

Group study

- † Divide into two groups, and each discuss their reactions to the *Song of Songs* passage.
- † Why does it belong in the Bible? Do you think you must read it only as an allegory of God's love or can it be said that God too delights in human sexuality? If you think the latter is true, is it also a part of being made in God's image as you discussed in Session One?
- † Let everyone get their dough or clay and make enough space for the group to spread out their newspaper, and put their board and dough on top of it.
- † The participants should experience moulding the dough for five minutes and be encouraged to enjoy the way it feels.
- † While one person reads aloud Luke 8.40–43, the others begin to shape their dough to express for themselves the woman's great pain and feeling of exclusion. Allow up to 20 minutes for this part of the exercise.
- † The reader should read aloud the rest of the story while everyone else continues with their dough to express the healing of the woman and her restoration to the community.
- † Still working with your dough, talk in twos about your

feelings while you heard about the woman and her healing. What did you feel? What do you feel about your experiences of sexuality, menstruation and society's taboos? Listen carefully and sensitively to one another and remember that confidentiality is the essence of group trust.

† In the main group discuss other areas of people's lives which cause them to be excluded from society. How is the physical nature of women recognized and treated in church? How might your closeness with other women and men be celebrated in a church service?

PRAYER

Sit together in a circle and put the shapes which you have moulded in the middle. Light a candle and put it among them. In silence, think about both readings for this session. Pray together:

O God, our beloved
born of a woman's body;
you came that we might look upon
you,
and handle you with our own hands.
Grant that we may so cherish one
another in our bodies
that we may also be touched by you,
Through the Word made flesh,
Jesus Christ, Amen.

You may wish to end with a kiss of peace, a hug, or with all holding hands in a circle as you say the Grace together.

PREPARATION FOR SESSION FIVE

Protecting the environment is a popular issue these days and everyone seems to want to be seen as "green". Before the session, cut out stories about the environment from recent newspapers, and bring them to the session. Collect any information you can from agencies working to protect the environment, like Greenpeace or Friends of the Earth. If you can, find out what raw materials the industries in your area use and what part of the world they come from. Also bring something you have made by hand to the session, some knitting, carving, sewing, modelling or something like that, so that you can talk about how the items were made.

SESSION FIVE

WOMEN AND THE ENVIRONMENT

AIM

In this session you will look at how women and men play a part in the stewardship of God's creation, and how God is revealed in creation.

[1]O LORD, our Lord,
your greatness is seen in all the world!
Your praise reaches up to the heavens;
[2]it is sung by children and babies.
You are safe and secure from all your enemies;
you stop anyone who opposes you.
[3]When I look at the sky, which you have made,
at the moon and the stars,
which you set in their places –
[4]what is man, that you think of him;
mere man, that you care for him?
[5]Yet you made him inferior only to yourself;
you crowned him with glory and honour.
[5]You appointed him ruler over everything you made;
you placed him over all creation;
sheep and cattle, and the wild animals too;
the birds and the fish
and the creatures in the seas.
[9]O LORD, our Lord,
your greatness is seen in all the world!

Psalm 8

Psalm 8 sets out the greatness of God and the dignity of human beings. (Note that "man" in this translation is one of the places mentioned in Session One where inclusive language is not used, but the Hebrew word used means "human being".) Yet this psalm is not primarily about the wonder of nature but about who is in control over it. Human beings are given responsibility for ruling nature (see verse 6), but if God's greatness is to be seen through it then it must be safeguarded and not abused.

GROUP STUDY

- † What picture is given of God and creation in Psalm 8?
- † Pool all the cuttings from the newspapers and try to sort them into topics such as water, animals, the atmosphere, the land and so on.
- † In twos or threes take some of the newspaper stories and discuss what the creation of God is in each. If the story is about something that has gone wrong, who has caused it? How might the situation be changed for the better? What would the cost be in money, changes to lives and traditions, and in other ways? Look again at the psalm and see how it fits with the issue you are discussing.
- † In the main group, discuss what the major industry is in your area. How does it relate to the issues you have been looking at in the small groups? Where is God's creative activity seen in that industry?
- † Put all your pieces of handiwork in the middle and each person describe in turn how they achieved it, what work was involved and what could have gone wrong in the making. Think about the universe, and as a group imagine from God's point of view how that creation was achieved, what labour went into it and what could have gone wrong with it. This exercise is an opportunity to try to "feel" how God might have felt and not an exercise in scientific accuracy!
- † Look again at your analysis of the local industry and begin to plan a church service, or part of one, to show your thinking about God's creation, human creation, and our responsibility towards the local, national and wider

environment. As you do this, think of ways to celebrate your partnership in creativity with God. Think too how to make people more aware how vulnerable our environment is. You could use such a service to show your work as a Bible study group to others.

Prayer

With your handiwork, the cuttings and anything else you have done today in the middle, pray together;

God our creator,
You have made us one with this earth,
to tend it and to bring forth fruit;
may we so respect and cherish
all that has life from you,
that we may share in the labour of all creation
to give birth to your hidden glory.
Through Jesus Christ, Amen,

Preparation for Session Six

Session six involves a group exercise. Decide among yourselves who is going to lead it so that he or she has time to prepare.

Before the session look at your local community and notice who brings home the money and how they earn it. Look at your own income if you have one. How do you use the power that your money gives you, in deciding what you will buy? Bring to the session any information you can find out about how both the country's and the world's wealth is distributed. (Try your local library: sometimes large atlases will show such information in map form.)

SESSION SIX

WOMEN AND JUSTICE

AIM

In this session you will look at God's demand for justice for the poor, which means more than people being equal and debts being paid, and at how we may help that justice in our local community and in the world.

6 The LORD says, "The people of Israel have sinned again and again, and for this I will certainly punish them. They sell into slavery honest men who cannot pay their debts, poor men who cannot repay even the price of a pair of sandals. 7 They trample down the weak and helpless and push the poor out of the way. A man and his father have intercourse with the same slave-girl, and so profane my holy name. 8 At every place of worship men sleep on clothing that they have taken from the poor as security for debts. In the temple of their God they drink wine which they have taken from those who owe them money.

Amos 2.6–8

9 Announce to those who live in the palaces of Egypt and Ashdod: "Gather together in the hills surrounding Samaria and see the great disorder and the crimes being committed there."

10 The LORD says, "These people fill their mansions with things taken by crime and violence. They don't even know how to be honest. 11 And so an enemy will surround their land, destroy their defences, and plunder their mansions."

12 The LORD says, "As a shepherd recovers only two legs or an ear of a sheep that a lion has eaten, so only a few will survive of Samaria's people, who now recline on luxurious couches."

Amos 3.9–12

1 Listen to this, you women of Samaria, who grow fat like the well-fed cows of Bashan, who ill-treat the weak, oppress the poor, and demand that your husbands keep you supplied with liquor! 2 As the Sovereign LORD is holy, he has promised, "The days will come when they will drag you away with hooks; every one of you will be like a fish on a hook. [3]You will be dragged to the nearest break in the wall and thrown out."

Amos 4.1–3

The prophet Amos was called by God to deliver warnings to the people round about and to call them to be a more just society. God reminds the people (Amos 2.9–11), that they were rescued and shown mercy and treated well but that they have perverted God's justice. In the three passages here, God warns the people of Israel, Egypt, Samaria and Ashdod that their injustices to the poor will lead to their own destruction. Amos (probably a sheep owner and not just a shepherd) from Tekoa, would have known about economic power. He would have known the system of reclaiming debt, and yet he would also know the command that the debtor must not be left completely destitute.

Group Study

† Listen together to the passage from Amos and make a list of the acts of oppression he mentions. Where can similar acts be seen today in your own community, your country and in the world? Look together at the preparation you did on money and its distribution.

† The next exercise is called an imaginary journey. It should last up to 20 minutes. The leader for this exercise will lead you through it but not participate in it in order to free the rest of you to join in fully. The leader should follow the exercise speaking clearly and calmly, and without rushing. It helps if he or she is relaxed too.

Leader: get the members of the group in a comfortable position. To help everyone get ready, lead them in this relaxing exercise (if they are lying down, adapt it accordingly):

"Gently allow your eyes to close. Place your feet flat beneath you, and feel them comfortably supported by the floor. Feel the seat of the chair take the weight of your legs. Let your back straighten; feel the pressure of the chair against it. Your shoulders are relaxed; your hands lightly rested on your lap. Allow your head to rise as you start to breathe in very slowly . . . and gently, slowly, out again. Your head is lifted upright and high; it takes no effort to hold it there. Breathe in again, gently, deeply . . . and slowly out again. Continue to breathe slowly and deeply, feeling more and more rested.

"Now, I want you to imagine you are somewhere public near here that you know quite well . . . Look around you at the buildings, the spaces, the trees if there are any . . . Notice the colours . . . Smell the smells and listen to the sounds . . . Now walk around and look at the other people there . . . Notice the variety of people you can see . . . Look at what they are wearing . . . What are they doing and saying? . . . Now you see Jesus walking slowly nearby . . . What is he wearing? . . . Who is he talking with? . . . What is happening? . . . What is Jesus saying? . . . [about 10 minutes' pause] Now you go to meet with Jesus . . . What does he say to you? . . . You watch him turn and walk away . . . Now you too walk back the way you came . . . Look around as you pass the places you have already been . . . [2 minutes' pause] Now it is time to return to this room . . . In your own time, open your eyes and when you are ready, get up slowly and sit back in the group."

Sit for a few minutes and recollect the experiences of your own imaginary journey. If you find it helpful, note down or draw some images to help you recall it. Get together in pairs and recount your journey to each other. Allow 5 minutes each without interruption. Listen to one another carefully. In large groups discuss what Jesus was saying to other people in your journey. What did Jesus say to you? How will you respond?

† In the main group discuss in what ways your church is involved in the struggle for justice. Is it making the situation better or worse? What little steps towards the vision for justice might you take as a group? Be practical and then decide to act!

Prayer

Pray for people who are oppressed in your local area, in your country and in the world, especially for victims of economic oppression. Pray together:

O God our deliverer
you cast down the mighty,
and lift up those of no account;
as Elisabeth and Mary embraced
with songs of liberation,
so may we also be pregnant with
your Spirit,
and affirm one another in hope for
the world,
through Jesus Christ, Amen.